Love God...Clean House...Help Others

Duane F. Reinert, O.F.M. Cap.

Paulist Press
New York/Mahwah, New Jersey

Cover/book design and interior illustrations by Nicholas T. Markell.

Library of Congress Cataloging-in-Publication Data

Reinert, Duane F., 1949–
    Love God—clean house—help others / by Duane F. Reinert.
       p.   cm.—(IlluminationBooks)
    Includes bibliographical references.
    ISBN 0-8091-3643-0 (alk. paper)
    1. Spiritual life—Christianity. 2. Twelve-step programs—Religious aspects—Christianity. I. Title. II. Series.
BV4501.2.R437   1996
248.4—dc20   96-5524
                                             CIP

Published by Paulist Press
997 Macarthur Boulevard
Mahwah, NJ 07430

Printed and bound in the
United States of America

Contents

IlluminationBooks

A Foreword

*I*lluminationBooks bring to light wonderful ideas, helpful information, and sound spirituality in concise, illustrative, readable, and eminently practical works on topics of current concern. Learning from stress; interior peace; personal prayer; biblical awareness; walking with others in darkness; appreciating the love already in our lives; spiritual discernment; uncovering helpful psychological antidotes for our tendency to worry too much at times; and important guides to improving interpersonal relations, are only several of the areas which will be covered in this series.

The goal of each IlluminationBook, then, is to provide great ideas, helpful steps, and needed inspiration in small volumes. Each book offers a new beginning for the reader to explore possibilities and embrace practicalities which can be employed in everyday life.

In today's busy and anxious world, Illumination-Books are meant to provide a source of support—without requiring an inordinate amount of time or prior preparation. Each small work stands on its own. Hopefully, the information provided not only will be nourishing in itself but also will encourage further exploration in the area.

One is obviously never done learning. With every morsel of wisdom each of these books provides, the goal is to keep the process of seeking knowledge ongoing even during busy times, when sitting down with a larger work is impossible or undesirable.

However, more than information (as valuable as it is), at the base of each work in the series is a deep sense of *hope* that is based on a belief in the beautiful statement made by Jesus to his disciples and in turn to us: "You are my friends" (Jn 15:15).

As "friends of God" we must seek the presence of the Lord in ourselves, in others, in silence and solitude, in nature, and in daily situations. IlluminationBooks are designed to provide implicit and explicit opportunities to appreciate this reality in new ways. So, it is in this spirit that this book and the other ones in the series are offered to you.   —*Robert J. Wicks*
General Editor, IlluminationBooks

Introduction

*W*e know that all things work for good for those who love God, who are called according to his purpose (Rom 8:28).

Early in life we did not have to worry about self-care. Parents fed, clothed, and sheltered us. Our caregivers nurtured and protected us.

Now we are responsible for caring for ourselves, but are still influenced by that early period. In the first few years, we learned from personal experience, and at a very deep level, whether our world is trustworthy or unpredictable, safe or dangerous, friendly or hostile, caring or cold. From that primal experience, my world is dif-

LOVE GOD
CLEAN HOUSE
HELP OTHERS

ferent from yours. We were cared for differently, and so now we each have our unique experience of needs, reactions, and feelings as we try to care for ourselves.

There are, however, common themes. The most self-sufficient adult feels the heart longing for affection and affirmation. None of us is completely self-sufficient. We have common fears as well as needs for safety and protection. None of us tolerates isolation, even self-imposed isolation, for any length of time and thrives.

The manner in which we care for ourselves, or neglect to do so, has its roots in our personal histories. Perhaps we have picked up bad habits along the way, such as neglecting entire dimensions of ourselves. Self-care involves paying attention to ourselves, getting to know ourselves and our needs. Too often we are our own worst enemies. We do not listen to ourselves. We do not hear what our personal history or our current experience tells us. We do not tune in to the music of our own beings.

When I was doing my doctoral research I had the privilege of getting to know many good people in the fellowship of Alcoholics Anonymous. One of the seasoned veterans of that group explained that the approach of A.A. was really rather simple: "Love God. Clean house. Help others."

Sure enough, after reading the basic text *Alcoholics Anonymous* or "Big Book" as it is affectionately called, and reviewing the 12 Steps, I could see that it truly boils down to three simple statements. Love God. Clean house. Help others.

Many do not realize that A.A.'s co-founder, Bill Wilson, drew heavily from the accumulated wisdom of Christianity when he articulated his understanding of the process of change. He summarized that process in the 12 Steps.

Wilson himself had a religious experience while he was in treatment for alcoholism and was given William James' *Varieties of Religious Experience* to assist him in interpreting it. Wilson was influenced both by that book and also by his membership in a dynamic Protestant religious movement. The goal of that movement, the Oxford Group, was to recapture the spirit of primitive Christianity. Wilson and his recovering alcoholic friends associated with that group for fellowship and support.

Now sober and converted, Wilson tried preaching the message of how to recover to other alcoholics. He quickly discovered his approach did not work. Other alcoholics, like Wilson himself in his drinking days, turned a deaf ear to preaching. So Wilson took a close look at himself and the process of conversion that he was currently engaged in, the process taught by the Oxford Group. He then took the core ideas, removed the religious language, and sculpted a spiritual program of change.

This book will follow the same simple outline. Love God, clean house, and help others. It will draw upon the living lessons of many people, gleaning kernels of wisdom from the experience of others. Not every thought will apply to you, so take what is helpful and leave the rest.

Participants in A.A. quickly learn that, although A.A.'s philosophy is simple, living the program is a day to day challenge. So it is with the thoughts in this book on self-care. Taking care of ourselves is a day to day process of putting rather simple ideas into practice.

If I learned one thing over the years, it is that self-care is not a solo endeavor. We simply cannot go it alone. God and others are intimately and essentially involved. The key is finding the proper balance.

One piece of wisdom has universal application: You may not be responsible for your problems, but you are responsible for what you do about them. No matter what our challenges, we may not be responsible for the predicament, but we surely can do something.

A Native American college student spoke rather elegantly to the idea of our responsibility for our actions. She had recently gone through a fight with her boyfriend, a disagreement that had continued for several days. Throughout the duration of the argument she refused to cook a meal for him at her apartment. She recounted how her grandmother used to take her aside in the kitchen and pass along wise teachings from her tribal ancestors.

"Child," her grandmother said, "when you prepare a meal for your family, be aware of what is in your heart. Whatever you bring within your spirit to the preparation of the meal flows through your hands and fingers and affects the food you prepare. You may be feeding your family anger, hostility, jealousy, or whatever is disturbing your heart. As you enter the kitchen," she advised, "cleanse yourself of all malice, and guard your thoughts. Be aware, when you handle the food, of love and good thoughts for those you will feed."

Such a mindful approach could help all of us in our task of self-care. Would that we could become more mindful of what we are fostering in our hearts! We would then become more aware of what we are feeding others. Perhaps we could choose to foster and to serve more peace, harmony, and love. Doing those things would require us to face ourselves honestly and become more attuned to our inner landscape.

Chapter One

"Love God!"

"What eye has not seen, and ear has not heard, and what has not entered the human heart, what God has prepared for those who love him," this God has revealed to us through the Spirit *(1 Cor 2:9–10)*.

Paradoxically, self-care begins with the recognition of our limitations. We are not God. As long as we cling to the illusion that we can take care of ourselves, we undermine the very ground on which we stand.

Take a few moments to think about it. Let's say I hold on to the notion that I can take care of myself, I can solve my own problems, I can do what I want, go where I

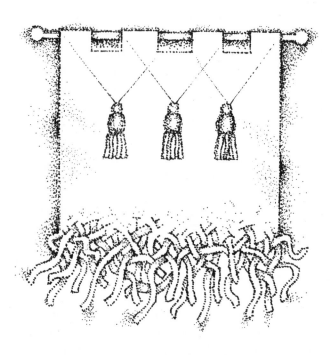

want, and be what I want to be. What a weight! If I rely only on myself and if my tapestry begins to unravel, where can I turn? What if my creation begins to crumble? If I am ultimately responsible, failures will crush me in the weight of despair.

Allowing God to be God, and allowing me to be creature—simultaneously weak and pitiful, yet created in God's image and likeness—is the simple, yet formidable task. More than once, beaten alcoholics have found their way to the rooms of Alcoholics Anonymous and stumbled over the idea of handing their lives over to the care of God. What does one do when there is no "God of one's understanding"? Time and again the advice has been to act as if you believe, or at least be open to the possibility of a power greater than oneself, and perhaps the gift of faith will be given.

More than twenty years ago popular preacher and theologian Father Robert L. McCreary addressed his fellow Capuchin-Franciscan friars on the topic of spiritual formation of young men entering religious life. He stressed that there is a fundamental, basic religious act that must be made. This act underpins any attempt at prayer. It underlies any other religious act a person performs to express one's relationship with God. That fundamental act he named the religious act of surrender.

He defined this act as "a surrender to God in such a way that one perceives that his [or her] surrender is accepted by God."[1] The friar further explained that an essential element of this act is that there is a living experi-

---

9

ence of relationship with God. Those who make this religious act of surrender utterly commend their hearts, their lives, their decisions to God. When they do so, this act forms a foundation on which the rest of their life is based. The relationship which flows from the religious act undergirds their sense that God accepts this surrender. In other words, when one makes this act, one perceives in it a personal relationship between oneself and God.

We stand before God and hand over our life with all its beauty and ugliness. In an act of faith, we offer all we are and sincerely believe that God accepts the likes of us. Father McCreary notes that Jesus made this act many times in his life. So convinced was Jesus of the importance of this that when he taught his disciples to pray, he included the petition to the Father, "your will be done, on earth as in heaven" (Mt 6:10). Near the end of his life, in his agony in the garden Jesus prayed: "not my will but yours be done" (Lk 22:42). In these words Jesus was offering to the Father the direction and purpose of his life. His final self-giving took place on the cross. He commended the very breath of life into the hands of his Father in his final act of surrender, "Father, into your hands I commend my spirit" (Lk 23:46).

On the cross Jesus gave his life to God in such a way that he understood it was accepted by his Father. The Father transformed that gift in the glory of the resurrection. The reward of fidelity in love was risen life.

The friar suggested that the act of surrender is the

same act that members of A.A. make when they turn their lives over to their Higher Power. Until this act of surrender is made at the depths of one's heart, there is a "holding back." I keep corners of my heart for myself. I do not entrust God with *all* of myself; I hoard a portion. I cling to what I name as mine alone. Until I can relax my grip enough to let go and hand over my very self to my creator, I play at being my own god.

This religious act of surrender is the foundation for prayer. Some people do not pray because the very foundation that undergirds prayer is not there. From a Christian perspective, there needs to be a basic sense that we are relating to the Lord God who manifested himself in Jesus Christ. We also must sense that Christ accepts us, warts and all.

Jesuit theologian Bernard Lonergan stated that humanity's highest achievement is falling in love with God. Why? Because once we fall in love with God, all is transformed. We stand on higher ground and can see from a perspective previously unknown and unimagined. Our values are placed on a new footing. We see things from a new perspective. We begin to understand our connection to everyone that God loves. The words of St. John begin to make sense when he says that anyone who says he loves God while at the same time hating his neighbor is a liar (1 Jn 2:4). We start responding in union with God. We start becoming what God created us to be.

But this "falling in love with God" is not just an

intellectual decision. It is much deeper than that. It is one thing to be able to talk about our belief system, to articulate and face our doubts, to have thought through what we believe in, and it is another thing to go into our room, close the door and kneel facing our God (see Mt 6:5–6). Karl Rahner said that one of the most important acts of witness to our faith is to kneel down where no one can see us because we then bear witness to ourselves that we believe in God.

Kneeling before the Lord in this way is an all-inclusive act: physical, mental, emotional, and spiritual. Our bodies, minds, and souls are united. We experience ourselves as an integrated whole. The opposite of self-care is experiencing ourselves as *dis*-integrated, divided, or fragmented.

Some of us are like the apostle Thomas who was told by other disciples of Jesus that the Lord is risen. They had witnessed his risen presence in their midst. Thomas replied that he would not believe without seeing. He wanted to put his hand in the nail holes; then the resurrection would be real. He wanted to put his hand in Jesus' side; then he would believe. Thomas wanted to touch. He wanted Jesus' human touch. When Jesus appeared again, he invited Thomas to touch because that was what Thomas needed. Like Thomas, some of us believe when we can touch, when we can see for ourselves.

The other side of the coin is also true. We also see when we believe. When we fall in love with God, things take on new meaning. We see things differently.

There is a new context. Our many and varied hopes are undergirded with hope.

A fellow therapist commented at a staff meeting that counseling a person who has no faith is a difficult task. Without faith in God, without belief in a personal and friendly ground of being, where does one find hope? If one relies only on oneself and one's fellow (and frail) humans, what happens when I cannot handle it anymore and what happens when those I counted on also walk away? Where do I turn? To what does a counselor appeal, to inspire confidence?

A young single mother approached me after a service during the season of Lent. She asked to speak privately. She admitted that she had neglected her faith since childhood. She had gone to confession and communion as a child but drifted away from her practice of faith. She explained that she began doubting God's existence in her early teen years. For several years God did not exist for her. Now she was beginning to experience a pull toward faith in God, even in the midst of her doubts. She truly desired such faith, but admitted that she felt confused. Sometimes she believed in God; sometimes the doubts were overwhelming.

This young mother obviously felt vulnerable and humbled as she tried to express her lack of confidence in God. Silence punctuated her story. Her head was bowed, her eyes focused on her hands fidgeting in her lap. Slowly she raised her head and with tender eyes said, "But faith is a gift, isn't it?" I nodded my assent. She released a deep sigh of relief.

What a relief when we are able to allow God to be God! A burden is lifted when we recognize that we are not responsible for giving ourselves the gift of faith, or engineering our own salvation. I am not God. I am responsible for some things, but I need wisdom to know where my responsibility ends and God's begins.

St. Francis of Assisi was a man who had a tender, affective relationship with God. However, the road to that relationship was long and rocky. He wrestled with God. He struggled to know himself.

As a young man Francis was restless. He filled his days and nights with friends, parties, and the delightful diversions of twelfth century wealthy teens. The frivolous activity gave way to the lure of knighthood and chivalry. With his father's money, he purchased the finest military equipment and joined the forces of Assisi. Reality hit hard as the romantic dreams of knighthood gave way to the harsh reality of being a prisoner of war.

A dream in that prison faced Francis with the question, "Who is it better to serve, the Master or the servant?"[2]

"Why, the Master of course."

"Then why, Francis, are you serving the servant?"

When Francis got out of his military predicament, he did nothing but search. He withdrew to caves and deserted places to reflect, to pray. He trusted God deeply, but the path was still not visible. What did God want him to do with his life? Where would he find peace?

One day during a time of prayer Francis heard an answer, but one that did not yet make sense.[3] "Francis! If you want to know my will, all that you once desired and loved you must now despise. What once you used to avoid and find repulsive will turn into sweetness and a great joy."

Even as a young man on the party circuit, Francis had a soft spot in his heart for the poor and outcast. He never neglected his civic duty in their regard. But now his search for the face of God brought Francis face to face with a leper.

Francis was repelled. Disgusting leper! His impulse was to give this man in his path a wide berth and proceed on his journey. Francis resisted the temptation to spur his horse away from the wretched outcast. This time Francis would not run from the leper, or from himself. This time he would stand still and face the repulsive leper who mirrored the dread and darkness Francis knew lurked inside himself.

Francis remembered the curious answer to his recent prayer and decided to take the Lord at his word. He dismounted and forced himself to wrap his arms around the leper. As the odor of rotting flesh flooded his senses, he bent and kissed the leper's hand and pressed a sack of alms into the hand. Francis' heart pounded and a rush of excitement shuddered his body. Before he knew it, he had mounted his horse and was riding away.

The Lord kept his word. What sweetness! What joy and peace filled his racing heart. Francis had met himself and also had embraced his Christ.

In that moment Francis' life was changed. He was now totally in the hands of God. From then on, Francis had no doubt that "not my will but thine be done" were his true words. Francis had no doubts that God would in turn provide for this little poor man of Assisi.

With reckless abandon Francis threw himself into serving the poor and into rebuilding and repairing churches. Men and women were drawn like magnets to this man's joy, energy, and serenity. Before long a brotherhood formed around the charismatic saint. Clare of Assisi also gathered women who were on fire with the spirit of Francis, a spirit bent on living the gospel simply and without gloss. In finding God, Francis found himself, found many brothers and sisters, and ultimately found himself intimately connected to all of God's creation.

Chapter Two

"Clean House!"

C*ast your care upon the* LORD, *and he will support you...(Ps 55:23).*

Self-care is not the same thing as pampering ourselves or indulging in self-gratification. Self-care involves an ongoing "house cleaning." We pick up bad habits, dysfunctional patterns, self-destructive tendencies, and all manner of clutter. Genuine self-love requires self-knowledge, calls for honest evaluation of weaknesses, and seeks a harmony and proper balance among the various dimensions of life.

In this chapter we will look at both "cleaning house," dealing with areas in ourselves that need to be changed, and also how we go about that task. In St. John's gospel, Jesus spoke about pruning the vines so they will bear more fruit (see Jn 15:1–5). Pruning is painful and must be done with care so the entire vine is not damaged in the process.

When we care for ourselves we recognize and value ourselves as creatures made in God's image and likeness. We allow God to be God, and we seek to love others as God loves them. We are then appropriately and peacefully connected—with self, creator, and fellow creatures.

Early in my counseling training I was assigned a female client, Bonnie. Bonnie was a petite young woman in her late twenties living with the effects of a crippling childhood illness. She walked with the aid of braces and canes. My initial impression, after a session or two, was that I was dealing with a pre-teen rather than a young woman. Her immaturity showed clearly in her speech and actions.

Bonnie was raised in a chaotic home. She was a victim of urban poverty, periods of neglect by her divorced parents, and sexual abuse by an older brother. Emotionally she was quite damaged.

Bonnie lived on the border of fantasy and reality. When the real world was too painful, she retreated to her rich imagination. At times it was difficult for me to sort out what was true from what was fantasy when she discussed her dealings with family and friends.

Up to that point I had not experienced anyone who used the type of psychological defense that Bonnie relied on to protect her emotional wounds. She was quite self-centered. The world revolved around her. She bragged about herself and gave me no indication of interest in others' feelings or opinions. She could not admit any fault or weakness.

But I learned something from Bonnie. I learned something about myself.

Many sessions were devoted to Bonnie's blaming an evil controlling woman for tearing her boyfriend away from her. Fred had moved to a neighboring state with this woman. Bonnie was convinced that if she could pry Fred away from the woman's clutches for a few moments, Fred would gladly choose Bonnie over his present girlfriend.

It was quite clear to me that Bonnie was mixing fantasy and fact. Fred had made his choice. I tried to shift our discussion to exploring with Bonnie if there could be any other reason that Fred had left the city. Is it possible that his feelings for Bonnie were not as strong as hers for him?

Bonnie was becoming noticeably agitated with this line of thought. Her bottom lip began to curl, her eyes teared up, and she shouted at me in anger, "You don't understand!" She proceeded to cry the first tears shed during a session since we had begun working together a few months earlier.

Like an oaf who had just caught on, I said quietly to her, "It would be too painful and devastating to admit that Fred has not chosen you, wouldn't it?"

"Yes," she whispered.

From that moment on, both Bonnie and I knew what the pain was about, even though she could not bring herself to look at it directly. It was just too much for her to face.

From Bonnie I learned to look at myself more honestly. I started becoming more curious about how I dealt with my hurts. I began to see how I used my own defenses to protect myself from the threatening world. Perhaps I did not go to the extremes she exhibited, but I also protect myself in egotistical and self-serving ways.

I remember the first time I submitted an article to a journal for publication. It was not accepted. The editor's letter had several paragraphs critiquing my work. When I first read it I felt personally attacked, as if the editor were ridiculing me. I had to get hold of myself and remind myself that the comments referred to the quality of my *work*, not the quality of my *person*! I forced myself to read the pages again to try to "hear" what they were saying. Despite my hurt feelings, I had to admit that the editor's comments were valid.

I learned from Bonnie that if I am going to be able to face any of my vulnerabilities, hurts, or weaknesses, I will have to ask myself if I am strong enough at the moment to deal with the issue. I learned how important it is to create a safe place to do so. Hitting things head on can be too brutal if I am already feeling vulnerable. From Bonnie I learned to name my own fears. From Bonnie I learned to appreciate how fragile we are and how in need we are of caring for ourselves with compassion.

When I feel affirmed, self-confident, and right with the world, it is easier to tackle challenging things. I can name my growing edges and not feel devastated. When I am feeling emotionally strong, I can review past events and recognize that I projected my own feelings or judgments on others. When I am strong I can admit my rationalizations and the ways I avoided people or used denial to ignore a problem.

However, what do we do when we are feeling like Bonnie? When we feel strong we can take a lot. When we feel weak and fragile, the smallest blow can knock us down for the count. Bonnie helped me see that seemingly small affirmations are vital. We need to find creative ways to bind our wounds and allow a stronger self to grow.

People who do not have a strong sense of self find it difficult to tolerate the thought of needing to improve or change. It feels quite threatening, something to escape as quickly as possible. But that sense of self can be nurtured, built up, and bolstered. In order to face the prospect of self-criticism and change, the core of myself must feel safe, loved, and appreciated. Perhaps that is the wisdom captured in the line from the *Desiderata* inscribed in St. Paul's Cathedral: "Beyond a wholesome discipline, be gentle with yourself."

St. Francis of Assisi went through a time of deep pain and found a rather creative way to address it.[4] During the time he was going through his conversion experiences, a rift was developing between himself and his father, Pietro Bernardone.

Pietro was a wealthy cloth merchant who wanted his son to make something of himself. He became increasingly incensed with his son's behavior. In Francis' enthusiastic response to what he thought God was calling him to do, he sold his father's precious cloth to finance the repair of churches. Francis gave money to the poor as if it were water. Pietro did not understand what was wrong with his son!

Pietro brought his son before the bishop of Assisi and demanded that Francis stop his activities and return his goods. Meanwhile it had become clear to Francis that he must give himself entirely to living the gospel. In front of the bishop of Assisi, Francis stripped himself of his clothes, piled them at the feet of his father, and said, "Up to now I have called you my father. Now I return to you my clothes and money—all the earthly possessions I received from you. From now on I will no longer say, my father Pietro Bernardone, but Our Father, who art in heaven!"

To Pietro's embarrassment, his son became a public beggar and a religious fanatic. He could not bear to see his son on the streets. If by chance they should meet, Pietro broke into wild fits of cursing. Francis was obviously pained by his father's rejection and devised an ingenious way to deal with it.

Francis asked an elderly beggar to accompany him.[5] If they chanced to meet Pietro, Francis would kneel down in front of his companion and plead, "Bless me, father!" The old man would dutifully bless his fellow beggar. Francis would then turn to his father and say, "See,

God has given me a father whose blessings will counter your curses."

Francis' solution was creative. Recognizing that reconciliation with his father was out of the question at the moment, but also recognizing the deep pain he felt in his father's rejection, Francis found a father figure to stand in and supply what he so deeply needed, his father's blessing.

Francis had two things going for him, his relationship with God and his creativity. His relationship with God and his solid faith in God's providential care for him provided a foundation from which he could deal with hurts. With this foundation in place, he could creatively generate options to care for himself.

Without a solid spiritual base, it is difficult to clean house. It's like sweeping a dirt floor. However, when we begin to get honest with ourselves and see ourselves clearly, it also can be disconcerting. We will see things we do not like. If we are feeling fragile, such introspection can shatter our confidence. Therefore, a solid faith in God is very important. It grounds us in the reality of our own goodness—because of God's goodness. Only when our feet are firmly planted in that assurance can we truly face ourselves and clean house.

Cleaning house is sorting through our faults, our limitations, our weaknesses. But too much focus on our frailties can drag us down, weaken our courage, and dampen our hope. Thus, it is good to take stock of a strength when we dredge up a fault. We may also need to remind ourselves that God's strength undergirds us.

We also keep in mind that the reason for cleaning house is for growth and improvement, and for deepening our relationships with God and others. It is for the purpose of caring for ourselves in the fullest sense of the word. Our understanding of care of ourselves is in the broader context of our understanding of where we fit in relation to God and God's creation.

The ancient practice of examination of conscience was devised and taught precisely for the purposes just mentioned. Properly prayed, the examination of conscience promotes a vital balance. Being conscious of God's love for us and his grace, we take a few minutes, perhaps ten to fifteen, to review our thoughts, words, deeds, and omissions over a particular span of time. Often the prayer is engaged in at the end of each day, so one reviews one's life over the past twenty-four hours, the period since the last examination of conscience. The prayer keeps in focus the fact that God is the very source of our activity. We reflect on how well we have responded to the gifts of his grace. The steps of this prayer are rather simple.

Step 1: Thank God. The first step of the examination of conscience is to remember we are in the presence of God and that our very lives are lived in the context of his gifts. We thank God as we become aware of the gifts. The goal of this step is to develop even greater sensitivities to the gifts around us and within us. And so, for example, we thank him for his sustaining love and all that keeps us in existence. We recall particular incidents in the course of the day that can be seen as treasures, times of beauty and peace, experiences of love and tenderness.

Step 2: Pray for honesty. Fortified by the sense of God's presence in the first step and graciously aware of the good gifts with which God surrounds our lives, we now ask God to help us be honest with ourselves. We pray for the ability to face ourselves and to view the events of the day with courageous honesty. We express the desire to see our true selves. We are asking for the courage to avoid excuses. We ask God to help us stay in the light of day and not flee to illusions or other defensive maneuvers.

Step 3: Review the day. In this step we review the thoughts and actions of our day. We do not just look for sins. We look at how we responded to God's grace. We look at both the positive and negative sides. We review our thoughts and the words we spoke. We review conversations. We admit our harsh judgments, our tendency to gossip, the unfair criticisms, and other forms of misuse of words. We review the words spoken in cooperation with God's grace—words of kindness, encouragement, and love. We review deeds. Were the acts we performed in keeping with our responsibilities and did we build up and promote goodness? Were our deeds malicious or harmful? We review our omissions. We consider what responsibilities we let slide.

Step 4: Ask forgiveness. Having become aware of the choices we made for good and the choices contrary to the good, we seek forgiveness and healing from God. This

step is an honest admission of our human frailties before God. This part of the prayer is our act of humility. If we were perfect, we would be God. Since we are not God, God does not expect perfection, just honesty. In this prayer we rejoice in the successes of the day and we seek forgiveness for failing to respond to God's grace in our choices.

Step 5: Set the goal. In this final step we make some decisions about how we will follow up on the above steps for the next twenty-four hours. We set some reasonable goals. We make some realistic plans on how those goals can be achieved, with God's help.

Cautions. Although the examination of conscience is a good and effective prayer when properly used, it also lends itself to distortions. A caution should be noted concerning the third step. If the third step occupies more time and energy than the other four steps, the prayer is being used incorrectly; it has become distorted. Remember, this is a prayer, not a court case against oneself. When we become detectives examining every corner of our lives for lurking sin, we have then developed a distorted and unhealthy introspection. We should be looking for more than sin. We should also be considering the positive responses to grace, the beauty of God working in us. And, finally, we should be careful that this exercise does not become a self-serving self-appraisal.

We examine our lives as members of the body of Christ, not just as individuals. We consider our connections with other members of that body and the head himself. We are not alone. No one comes to God without others. No one makes spiritual progress alone; God's grace and the help of others are intimate players in our spiritual and religious lives.

The above steps of the examination of conscience can be "general" or "particular," depending on what we hope to accomplish. The general examination of conscience is just as I outlined it above. We look at the general or broad strokes of the day. But we can also use the same basic framework to focus on a particular issue. For example, a spouse could focus on developing a greater sensitivity and responsiveness to his or her partner. Then he or she would make a particular examination of conscience at regular intervals to reflect on progress in that specific area.

The traditional suggestion is to make the particular examination of conscience three times a day, upon rising, at noon, and before retiring. This keeps the topic in one's awareness on a regular basis.

The particular examen goes through the same five steps. The spouse gives thanks for the many gifts God has given in that particular area of life, asks God's help in order to face honestly the recent events, reviews actual behaviors, requests forgiveness for failing to respond to the promptings of God's grace, and makes resolutions for the period until the next examen.

St. Ignatius of Loyola advocated the general and particular examination of conscience and developed those ancient prayer forms. He suggested we write down the goals and progress we make from day to day or week to week, a practice encouraged by current self-help workbooks.

St. Ignatius is adamant in warning that the examination of conscience is a prayer form. It is not a technique for stoic self-mastery. It is not a path to spiritual self-consciousness or self-pride. It is prayer. The examen can be a prayerful and structured way of getting in touch with our inner selves.

St. Francis of Assisi recognized that we can do violence to ourselves by acting contrary to our conscience, by losing our integrity and not being true to ourselves. Acting contrary to our deepest sense of what is right creates a tension; it creates a divided self.

The Mirror of Perfection, an early source of the life of St. Francis, relates a revealing story of the saint challenging a fellow friar who wandered about with a gloomy face. The saint asked him why he was making such a public show of his sorrow for his sins. He suggested he work out his guilt with God, ask pardon, and get on with his life![6]

Francis had a sense of the pain we put ourselves through when we violate our own conscience, when we disturb our own peace of mind. Thomas of Celano, in *The First Life of St. Francis*, remarks that Francis was not ashamed to admit his faults and to confess his failings publicly. If he were angry or had unkind thoughts about a person, Francis would admit his fault and seek forgiveness. Thomas says, "His conscience...would not let him rest until it had gently healed the wound in his heart."[7]

We generally think that our harsh words, our unkind actions, our snide comments hurt others. We recognize the damage we do to the target of our vitriolic outbursts. Rarely do we sense the damage we do to ourselves. Francis perceived there was a "wound in his heart" caused by his attack, and even by an evil but unspoken thought. The selfish act of unkindness created a wound. The violation of his true self tore at his very core. By confessing his fault, Francis bound the wound of his divided self.

Chapter Three
More House Cleaning

Y ou cleanse the outside of cup and dish, but inside they are full of plunder and self-indulgence. Blind Pharisee, cleanse first the inside of the cup, so that the outside also may be clean (Mt 23:25–26).

There are many rooms in our house that may need cleaning. We may have thrown our physical needs into the basement of neglect. We may have stuffed the back corners of our closets with negative emotions and neglected our affective life. And the front parlor where we entertain our guests may have collected furniture that is not very functional.

Christianity values the human body. We are not

disembodied spirits; souls without bodies are incomplete. We believe that our God turned his face to us in the person of Jesus by taking on human flesh. Because of this belief, we have had a tradition of reverence for the body and valuing it as the "temple of the Holy Spirit," as St. Paul puts it (1 Cor 6:19).

As we grow to understand and appreciate our human nature, including the physical body, we deepen our faith. The more we understand ourselves, the more we understand our God. After all, we are created in God's own image.

During the first few centuries of Christianity's existence, the church encountered religious movements that had a deep mistrust of anything physical, including the human body. Although the church steered a path away from these heretical extremes, it has still felt their influence. Every now and then negative attitudes about the body rise to the surface.

St. Paul espoused a more positive view. Although he recognized that our human nature is weak and prone to sin, he believed we could triumph. Using the image of an athlete, he suggested that a Christian could train to win the race (1 Cor 9:24–27; 1 Tim 4:7), disciplining the body to function as God created it.

If we maintain a New Testament orientation, our self-care in the physical realm will avoid a pessimistic and individualistic focus. We will seek to balance health and overall well-being with an asceticism that honors the body and reverences it. The body is an integral part of our humanness. We nourish the body with the eucharist, the body of Christ; we live and die in union with Christ, rising to a new life as his people.

At times in the history of Christian spirituality, there have been exaggerated emphases on self-denial and subduing the body's passions, suspicion of sexuality and marriage, extreme moralism, or the belief that certain sins cannot be forgiven. Occasionally the body, with all of its desires and passions, has been seen as an obstacle to be tamed so the soul can rise to God in holiness.

Thomas of Celano tells a story in *The Second Life of St. Francis* about Francis, near the end of his life and quite ill, seeking counsel from one of his brothers.[8] Francis' conscience was bothering him. He was torn between easing the demands on his body in response to his illness, and inflicting his usual rigorous discipline.

The brother wisely questioned Francis, "Tell me, if you will, Father, with how much diligence did your body obey your commands when it could?"

"It was obedient in all things," Francis replied.

"Where then, Father, is your generosity, where are your kindness and discretion? Is this a worthy way to repay faithful friends, to accept a kindness willingly, but when the giver is in need not to repay him as he deserves? What could you have done up till now in the service of Christ your Lord without the help of your body?"

Francis had to agree. He thanked the brother for the wise advice. The saint then addressed his own body,

"Rejoice, brother body, and forgive me." He then promised his body he would listen to its complaints.

It seems obvious that self-care involves proper care of the body as well as the spirit. Such things as exercise, a healthy diet, and proper rest are common-sense elements in the care of our body. These are simple to identify, but hard tasks to pursue consistently!

For persons enjoying relatively good health, finding exercise opportunities are not difficult. Finding the time and committing ourselves to an exercise program is the challenge. To jump into an activity that we find tedious will insure a quick conclusion to our efforts. The prospect of engaging in exercise on a regular basis increases if it is something we enjoy. So giving some thought to what appeals to us is an important first step.

Some find brisk walks or jogging quite satisfying because they can delight in the flowers and trees, feel the breeze on the face, and be stimulated by and feel a part of nature's activity—feeling in sync with the pulse of creator and creation. Others find that a health or athletic club affords the opportunities they enjoy, whether it is exercise machines, weights, or competitive sports. Any number of aerobic exercise programs have been devised to suit the taste of many.

Other types of physical outlets, while no substitute for vigorous exercise, can express creative and spiritual dimensions of ourselves as well. Yoga, for example, can provide both a way to release physical tension as well as an opportunity to become focused and pray. Dance, art, crafts and other creative activities can be physical outlets for self-expression that are satisfying and life-giving.

Our emotional well-being and physical activity are closely related. Too often we do not appreciate the importance of physically expressing emotionally significant dimensions of our lives. Ritual is the name we give to the celebration of these important occasions. Ritual can be as simple as a couple consistently having their morning cup of coffee together on the sun porch as an expression of their commitment to each other.

Church and society ritualize such important events as marriage, the birth of a baby, transition to adulthood, and death through weddings, christenings, confirmations, and funerals. Ritual is simply a ceremony to celebrate and formalize a meaningful event.

Finding ways to ritualize key events can aid in personal and family transitions and help reduce tensions and psychological stress. Families, for example, often ritualize such events as birthdays and wedding anniversaries. The ritual can be simply singing "Happy Birthday," or it could be more elaborate, involving symbolic objects, ceremonial actions, and prayers.

Other important family events could also benefit from ritualizing, such as a child's leaving home for college or getting his or her first apartment. The occasion of a promotion at work, a transfer, or retirement could also be ritualized. Some of these events are stressful, not only for the one obviously affected, but for the entire family. Physically celebrating or ritualizing these events can provide an outlet to express the emotions that are not captured in words alone. Ritual can provide satisfying closure to experiences that defy words.

Another area that can be a challenge is dealing with unpleasant emotions. We can get very hard on ourselves and blame ourselves for having negative feelings. In those moments we discount the creation God would have us be; we only see the tarnish that hides the shine.

As we squarely face ourselves, we must make a distinction between our decisions, which have moral content, and feelings, which just are. We are not responsible for our feelings. Feelings are involuntary reactions. Yet we have a tendency to get down on ourselves for experiencing negative feelings: loneliness, sadness, depression, anger, and fear.

Anger is a good example. Anger is experienced by some as a sinful emotion. They seek to hide it or deny it exists. A thin veneer of "nothing's wrong" masks the deeper emotion.

But anger is simply an emotion. It is a feeling that is trying to tell us something. Anger is a signal, not a sin. What we *decide* to do in response to our angry feelings has moral content. But the feelings themselves are neither right nor wrong.

The letter to the Ephesians counsels, "Be angry but do not sin; do not let the sun set on your anger, and do not leave room for the devil" (Eph 4:26–27). The scriptures recognize that the emotion of anger will flare up, and they warn us to deal with it forthrightly so that we are not stuck in a hostile state. Even Jesus experienced angry feelings on various occasions (Mk 3:5; 10:14; Mt 15:7; 16:23; 23:13–36; Jn 2:15–17). His anger led to constructive action. The fire of his anger was neither ignored nor fanned out of proportion, nor was it "stuffed" to form deeper resentments.

The Hebrew scriptures are full of rich interactions between individuals and God, including angry ones. At times in scriptures we see prophets wrestling with God, questioning him, as Jacob did. They had a sense that God could be dealt with openly. For many of us, the tendency is to assume that we have to "make nice" to approach God.

I wonder if God would not like to say to us at times, "Come on, get real! Tell me what's really on your mind." Think about it. God knows the anger within us, but hears us voicing, "Sweet and loving Jesus, you are so gentle and kind." Don't we realize that God knows about the rough jagged edges of our hearts?

What would happen if I voiced my lament just as I feel it? Would God think any less of me? What does he think of me when I try to hide my true self from him? Isn't it a bit like Adam and Eve running and hiding from God in the garden of Eden? But if God is not big enough to take my anger, who is?

Other feelings, such as loneliness, sadness, and fear, are also signals. If we become attentive to our emotional landscape, we may be able to come up with creative ways of dealing with our negative emotions. Where is the loneliness coming from? Is there someone I can talk to, or something that I could do, to help fill the emptiness I feel? At the very least I could think of the people who would want to be with me if they could.

When we are feeling depressed and low, we usually feel like doing nothing. If we follow our feelings, little is accomplished. We need to make a *decision* to act, to busy ourselves, to get involved in our own healing.

Love, also, is not just feelings; it is a decision. Sometimes we do not feel very loving, but we can still decide to love. Pete was a middle-aged client who had been married for a number of years. He told me that he and his wife had tried marital counseling in the recent past. They mutually agreed to terminate the marital counseling because it was not providing the expected results. Both realized their individual issues were blocking progress in the relationship. Seeking individual counseling seemed to be a reasonable alternative.

Pete questioned whether he loved his wife. He was not at all sure he wanted to continue in the marriage. Looking back, Pete recognized that neither the courtship nor the marriage was ever sparked with wild passion. Theirs was a comfortable friendship that grew into marital companionship. Over the years a couple of children arrived, work and home life became routine, and some maladaptive communication patterns set in.

Pete began examining his side of the marital relationship. He came to see clearly that he had fallen into a habit of saying what he thought his wife wanted to hear.

He had made some assumptions and had acted upon them. He assumed his wife could not handle the truth. He assumed she would make life quite unpleasant if he voiced an opinion contrary to hers. He interpreted her managing the household schedule, child rearing, and other responsibilities as exercising control. He assumed she would actively take more control of his life if he did not continue to please her by saying whatever he thought she wanted to hear.

In one of our sessions it became quite clear to me that Pete's lack of assertiveness and his perception of his wife being controlling was largely due to his fear of losing her if he did not please her. He was taking responsibility for how she felt and had an exaggerated sense of her fragility.

Since he was not sure he wanted to continue the marriage, I suggested he might test the waters. What if you say what you really think? What if you are honest? Perhaps she won't like what she hears and will call the marriage quits. In that event, you would know that if you both are honest you cannot live with each other. If you do not try to please her but speak your truth, and your honest words are received favorably, perhaps there is something worth preserving in the marriage.

For a time, Pete spoke his thoughts and feelings clearly to his wife. It was not easy. He struggled with the old feelings, the self-imposed "requirement" that he had to please her in order for him to be liked or accepted. He still tended to take responsibility for her feelings, but struggled to make clear distinctions for himself. When his wife expressed negative emotions, Pete tended to fall into the old trap of trying to smooth things over, trying to guess and to say what he thought would make things better for her.

On one occasion when he described an event in which he clearly was not responsible, I asked him, "Did you kick the dog?" This question became his mantra. Whenever he began feeling guilty for the way his wife was feeling or acting, he would ask himself if he was responsible. "Did you kick the dog, Pete?" If he had done nothing to warrant her reaction, he could tell himself that she, not he, would have to sort things out. He began to realize that he was not responsible for every feeling, every reaction his wife experienced. He could mentally separate her issues or problems from his.

Pete discovered that he had developed similar maladaptive patterns of communication at work. With his newfound way of relating to his wife functioning rather well, he decided to be a little more assertive at work. He decided that rather than just going along with the ideas the boss suggested, he began explaining alternatives that seemed more realistic or useful. Within a few months, Pete reported that his ability to speak forthrightly to his boss was paying off. The boss began looking to Pete for advice. In turn, Pete began encouraging co-workers to be less timid in speaking up to superiors when they had valuable suggestions or comments.

By the time Pete decided to terminate counseling, he not only established a more effective pattern of communication, he had rekindled with his wife some of the warmth and loving feelings of their early years together. He made a renewed commitment to his wife. The children sensed the stability of their parents' relationship and responded with fewer behavioral problems.

In his counseling sessions with me, Pete initially identified the personal issues he wished to address. He was not assertive. He guessed and spoke what he thought others, especially his wife, wanted to hear. But when Pete addressed those issues, he found that relationships changed and became healthier. In caring for himself he provided a context for a more stable family life and a more healthy pattern at work.

Chapter Four
"Help Others!"

 No one has ever seen God. Yet, if we love one another, God remains in us, and his love is brought to perfection in us *(1 Jn 4:12)*.

"Help others!" hardly seems to be related to self-care. But it is. I heard an anecdote several years ago, attributed to the prominent psychiatrist Dr. Karl Menninger. It is one of those stories that is in keeping with his spirit, and if it is not true, it ought to be.

Dr. Menninger, who was frequently called upon to speak, was asked by a member of the audience what initial advice he would give to a person who felt depressed. Reportedly his answer was not to see a mental health professional for counseling, nor turn to a psychiatrist for medication. His advice was, "Go help someone."

When we are experiencing the ordinary blues, focusing on "poor me" can add to the darkness. When we transcend ourselves and get interested in someone else's need, paradoxically we feel much better. Helping others builds up ourselves. There is nothing quite like the satisfaction and the joy one gets in making a difference in the life of another.

This was brought home to me pointedly, and many times over, in a rather unlikely setting. A number of years ago, Glenn Dale Hospital was a long-term facility caring for the destitute of Washington, D.C. Most patients admitted to that hospital could expect to live out their remaining days there.

When I was in theological training in preparation for ordination to the priesthood, this hospital was one of the places I volunteered to visit to gain my necessary practical ministry skills. In August of the beginning of my second year of theology, I was scheduled to accompany the hospital's chaplain, Father Fred, to the facility. This chaplain was also one of my theology professors and an instructor in practical ministry skills.

The atmosphere of the hospital was a jolt to this farm boy from Kansas. I remember the first day I walked with Father Fred through the front doors of the hospital. My task that Sunday morning was to help other volunteers round up patients in wheelchairs and on carts and wheel them down to the chapel for mass.

To describe that late August morning as hot and humid would be an understatement. The building was old, not air conditioned, and the corridors were heavy with the smell of antiseptic. I walked beside Father Fred down the patient-lined halls. He introduced me to this patient and to that one. But I was not yet meeting people. I was overwhelmed by missing limbs, crippled bodies, foul smells, and cries of pain in the background.

My stomach began to protest, and my head felt light and dizzy. Embarrassed, I turned to the chaplain and told him I was about to faint. He enlisted a kind nurse who gave me saline solution and ushered me to an empty bed. I stared at the ceiling, duly humbled. On my first day of hospital ministry, I was flat on my back. Subsequent days went better; there was nowhere to go but up!

In this warehouse of people waiting for death were several who were about to teach me some memorable lessons about living. One lesson had to do with caring for oneself by helping others.

Eliza Ann Dobson was the daughter of an old-fashioned black preacher. She would sit reading her Bible Sunday mornings and would greet the Catholic volunteers as they wheeled patients to chapel for mass. Ms. Dobson was not a stranger to anyone, patient, staff, or volunteer. Now and then she had her down days, but she knew how to get beyond herself and her blues by reaching out to others.

Ms. Dobson was struck with multiple sclerosis later in life than most. At the age of fifty-one, this elevator operator who had worked at the Internal Revenue Service building experienced her first symptoms. Ten years later, Miriam Ottenberg wrote an August 8, 1976, story for *The Washington Star* on Ms. Dobson and recounted the patient's first experience of the disease, "My feet got stubborn on the floor. I couldn't move them."[9]

After several visits to specialists, Ms. Dobson learned her diagnosis. Her illness claimed her mobility and her finances. Eventually Dobson arrived at Glenn Dale Hospital. At the age of sixty-one Dobson was told by her nurse that she could no longer tool through the halls in her wheelchair as she was accustomed to do. With limited exceptions, she was confined to bed. It was then that Ms. Dobson decided to write a song and get it published. She would earn some money for multiple sclerosis research.

Gathering ideas from her bible, she fashioned the words and hummed a tune. In a few short months it was ready. She located a minister who would take her audiotape, straighten out a few flaws in her verse, score the music, and get it published. He returned with a sheet of music, Ms. Dobson's completed three-verse spiritual, "Fret Not."

Ms. Dobson sold the sheet music for a dollar a copy. Fellow patients bought it. Hospital staff bought it. So did visitors. Ms. Dobson would sing her song at services in the hospital and more people bought copies.

The National Capital Chapter of the National Multiple Sclerosis Society sponsored a picnic that summer. Ms. Dobson arrived in the wheelchair the Society had purchased for her a long time ago. She presented her check for multiple sclerosis research, handing over the proceeds of the sale of five hundred copies of her song.

When asked if she couldn't use the money to supplement her small pension, Ms. Dobson replied: "I could die today or tomorrow and maybe they'll find a cure next week. Maybe that little $500 will help save somebody's baby. That's the way I feel about it."

The final verse of her song says it another way:

> Someday, somewhere, every thing is sweet and
> fair.
> No more pain and misery.
> We will be welcome up there
> If for Christ we have lived
> And service have giv'n
> Then we'll go home and get our crowns.

There is no doubt that Ms. Dobson was on a mission. She helped herself by helping others. She had a purpose much bigger than herself. In that purpose she found meaning and strength. She had a reason to live and something special to give.

People would have been able to understand if Ms. Dobson would have kept her money and spent it on herself. After all she had suffered a lot. She deserved it, one could argue. But Ms. Dobson's real joy was the thought that her gift might "save someone's baby."

I think of other patients at Glenn Dale when I think of helping others. I think of them because we so often get caught up in the mistaken belief that we have nothing to offer. But the magnitude of our gift has nothing to do with the giving. The fact that we give is what counts.

Leroy was a young man, perhaps in his thirties, who was a quadriplegic as a result of an accident. His body was twisted and deformed, so he could not comfortably use a wheelchair. A cart was his perch most days. He was propped up with pillows. His neck and upper chest muscles were well defined from years of surveying the world from his gurney.

When I met Leroy he was a cheerful, simple man. As any young man, Leroy had dreams for his future. But most dreams were unrealistic due to his physical condition. That did not stop him from being in the thick of socializing at the hospital.

Leroy regularly attended mass, prayer services, discussions, and celebrations. If there were people gathered, Leroy wanted to be there. Leroy expressed his joy and excitement beyond customary smiles and laughter. When he became enthusiastic, his limbs would begin to thrash, and he would erupt with a distinctive laugh.

Leroy enjoyed music. Although he couldn't carry a tune in a bucket, nor read the words of songs, Leroy's unmistakable drone would accompany congregational singing.

A volunteer brought him a harmonica. Leroy was delighted with the instrument. If it were placed on the gurney in the right spot, he could grab it with his mouth and blow some notes. Before long Leroy fancied that he had mastered the instrument enough to bring it to church and accompany the folk choir.

Fellow patients and volunteers were aware of Leroy's debut. All were prepared. The song began and Leroy joined in with his harmonica. Amid the discord was deep joy. Leroy's body thrashed with excitement. His eyes sparkled and the harmonica dropped to the cart as Leroy's mouth burst into smiles and laughter. The whole room joined him in enjoying his gift of "music."

Patients and volunteers alike loved seeing Leroy's simple and straightforward zest for life. Leroy's gift was not his musical talent, but his sincere and genuine joy in the little things of life. In his presence one could not ignore the smallest of blessings.

His simple gifts and enthusiasm for life were returned many times over. People were drawn to Leroy and, in turn, gave him encouragement and support needed to tolerate the limitations thrust upon him by his life circumstances.

Millie and Harold were another pair who taught much. The couple had been married many years and were still together in the hospital for their final days. Once a fairly prosperous lawyer, Harold was now senile and poor. Harold was in good physical health for his age; Millie was bedfast and frail but mentally she was still quite sharp.

Millie made arrangements with the hospital personnel to have Harold brought down from his third-floor room to have dinner at her bedside once each week. Week in and week out the ritual took place. Harold had no idea who this woman was, or why he was there. Millie was undaunted. She made conversation and gave a wonderful gift of inspiration to all who learned of this weekly event.

Millie had made a commitment to Harold years ago "until death us do part." We can only imagine the pain she felt at seeing her bright and dashing husband deteriorate to the point of not recognizing his wife. But from her perspective, this was all part of the deal. And Millie, through her bedfast generosity, touched more hearts than she knew.

Once a week she reached out with tender care. Harold still needed her love, even though his ability to appreciate her kindness was severely limited. But Millie knew, and that was what really counted. She could hold her head high, a woman of integrity. Her heart was pure and undivided; she was a personification of serenity.

Millie's ritual of care for Harold expressed her love and fidelity. She was peaceful knowing she was being true to herself and to her calling from God in marriage. But some of us have deep hurts that make such responses difficult. We get stuck and find it hard to look beyond ourselves.

Alcoholics Anonymous has something to teach us here. Some people are hurting and are floundering aimlessly in search of healing balms. Unfortunately alcohol and drugs make fast friends, but eventually turn on the user, viciously biting back like testy dogs.

Ernest Kurtz has written an article on why

Alcoholics Anonymous works and offers an insight into its wisdom.[10] Kurtz observes, as do most people who deal with alcoholics, that alcoholics develop rather firm systems of denial. They have a difficult time admitting they have a problem with alcohol.

Kurtz suggests that it is evident that there is a great deal of shame underlying their denial. He theorizes that alcoholics, at root, feel they are fundamentally flawed. Deep down they suspect they are utter failures.

But these feelings are too much to handle in conscious awareness. So, psychological defenses kick in. The feelings of shame and failure are blocked in an elaborate system of denial. As a defense, alcoholics deny they *need* alcohol. They deny they are hooked. "I don't drink because I *need* to," they say. "I can quit any time. I just *want* to drink." They also do not want help. "I don't *need* anyone. I can do it *myself*."

A.A. addresses this twofold denial of need, according to Kurtz. It asks people to admit they are alcoholics—to introduce themselves at A.A. meetings by their first name and say "I am an alcoholic."

A.A. draws on ancient Christian wisdom. The Christian doctrine of original sin is a theological expression for admitting that we all are flawed. We are limited. If we deny our flaws and say we are not sinners, we are taking a stance of pride. We make ourselves gods. To be humble is to be not-God, a sinner. Our usual way of denying our limitations is not directly saying, "I have no limitations." Rather, we usually express it by denying a need.

The alcoholic, for example, denies a need for alcohol and a need for others.

A.A. asks alcoholics to admit the need for others by placing them in a position where they are needed by other alcoholics, and are needed precisely and only as alcoholics. To say "I am an alcoholic" admits of a twofold need. It admits I am limited. But alcoholics also learn from experience that to be limited is to be real. Precisely as limited and broken, alcoholics can truly help one another. In the helping, they get out of the pit of self-doubt and confirm by experience their basic goodness. They transcend the bruised and brittle self.

By helping others we learn that, deep down, we have something good to give. We learn that our suspicions that we are fundamentally flawed, that we are not worthwhile, or that we are failures are wrong. We learn by experience that precisely because of our limitations we are needed. One alcoholic listens to another alcoholic because each "has been there."

When we try to help and see that we have an impact, we learn we are valuable. In our brokenness we have helped others deal with their brokenness. From experience we learn that we can get beyond our deepest unspoken fears that we are worth nothing.

The Christian pattern of the cross is evident here. Christ "did not regard equality with God something to be grasped," the letter to the Philippians states. "Rather, he emptied himself, taking the form of a slave, coming in human likeness;" (Phil 2:6-7), becoming, in a sense, not-

God. Being as we are, he embraced the cross, the symbol of degradation. "He humbled himself, becoming obedient to death, even death on a cross" (Phil 2:8).

Jesus did not embrace either humanity or the cross because *he* wanted to, but because *someone else—* God, his Father—wanted him to. And it did not feel particularly rewarding. In fact, he prayed in the garden "My Father, if it is possible, let this cup pass from me; yet, not as I will, but as you will" (Mt 26:39). He struggled, as all humans do, to embrace the will of his Father. He felt alone and abandoned. On the cross Jesus cried out, "My God, my God, why have you forsaken me?" (Mt 27:46).

Jesus was going through all of this for us, and in union with God, his Father. On the cross he affirmed his self-giving, "Father, into your hands I commend my spirit" (Lk 23:46). Jesus' self-giving was transformative. God raised him from the dead. The pattern of Jesus, the pattern of the cross and resurrection, is the pattern of his followers. It is our pattern.

For our own self-giving to be transformative, the act cannot be self-serving. It must be in keeping with God's will. In other words, if we are giving out of self-serving motives, the giving is not transformative. The giving must truly be *for* the other. Our hearts must be pure.

If we give of ourselves in that spirit—for others and in union with God's will—we experience reflexively our own goodness. In these moments we learn from experience that we are not fundamentally flawed; we experience ourselves as God created us, fundamentally good.

A similar insight is expressed in the book of the prophet Isaiah. In chapter 58 God reveals through the prophet the true fasting God requires of his people. It is not just a religious practice. True fasting releases those unjustly imprisoned, feeds the hungry, finds shelter for the homeless, and breaks the yoke of oppression. If you do those things, "then," says the prophet, "your light shall break forth like the dawn, and your wound shall quickly be healed" (Is 58:8).

Helping others is not just something that God commands us to do out of a sense of duty. Rather, helping others heals our wounds. When we help others our goodness shines like the light of dawn.

At times others help us in ways we can never repay. If God is love, then their gratuitous aid is a sign of that love. Perhaps we can never directly repay those who have made our path in life smoother, but we can "repay" by finding the ones who need *our* self-giving.

Helping others is an important dimension of self-care because it ties into our reason for being, our sense of purpose in life, our value as a creature. In our personal pains, isolation, and alienation we can experience a nagging self-doubt that would have us believe, "I am dirt." But when we connect with another in our mutual pain and try to help, we also connect in the healing and the growth. "It is in giving that we receive," the Peace Prayer of St. Francis states. It is a paradox that must be experienced to be believed.

Epilogue

*L*ook at the birds in the sky; they do not sow or reap, they gather nothing into barns, yet your heavenly Father feeds them. Are not you more important than they? (Mt 6:26).

Simplicity is itself a key to self-care. Our culture spreads the message that happiness is tied to acquiring more and better things. Our children are indoctrinated into the culture of consumption through clever ads and peer pressure. They are taught to need the "right" breakfast cereals, toys, and name-brand clothes.

Linda inadvertently got caught up in this treadmill of needs. She was a single woman in her mid-twenties when her mother died and left a modest amount of money. Since Linda had a good job, she decided to purchase her own home.

Linda once remarked to me that the most important part of the Sunday paper was the myriad of ads and sale fliers stuffed between the sections of printed news. Linda loved to shop. She had a wallet filled with credit cards—department store cards, as well as the major cards—and she used them.

Her needs multiplied. The house needed new furniture, drapes, and other appointments. Linda needed clothes, shoes, and accessories for work. She needed reliable transportation, so she traded in her old car for a newer model.

Soon Linda was deep in debt. Keeping up with monthly payments—house, car, insurance, credit card minimums—quickly became a high-pressure task. She took on a second job in a retail business.

Before long, Linda was working seven days a week. Some days she put in twelve to fourteen hours. The very things she "needed" in order to be truly happy were sapping the life out of her. She was physically drained from the constant demands of both jobs, and was feeling depressed and anxious with all the pressure from financial worries. She had become a slave to the debts that arose from her "needs."

Finally, her fiancé pointed out the madness of all this and suggested that things did not have to be this way. She awoke as if from a mindless daze. Somehow she had not been aware that by responding to subtle and creeping "needs," she was creating a destructive situation for herself.

Linda admitted she had gotten lured into a vicious cycle that eventually made her a slave to credit institutions. Now that she awoke and could see the pattern of mindless consumption, she could begin the task of simplifying her needs. After her debts were reduced to manageable size, Linda looked like a new person. She no longer had that depressed and weary look. She returned to working only one job and found some time to live.

By simplifying her life, she took a giant step toward caring for herself. Initially she had to make a conscious effort to look at her life and recognize what was happening in order to put it back on track again.

Self-care begins when we step back and assess our circumstances. What do I need to do in order to better love God, clean house, and help others?

Notes

1. Robert L. McCreary, O.F.M. Cap., "Helping Our Young Men Make the Religious Act" (unpublished manuscript).

2. See "Legend of the Three Companions," trans. Nesta de Robeck, in *St. Francis of Assisi: Writings and Early Biographies, English Omnibus of the Sources for the Life of St. Francis*, ed. Marion A. Habig (Chicago: Franciscan Herald Press, 1972), pp. 894–895. (Hereafter cited as *Omnibus*.)

3. Ibid., pp. 900–902.

4. Ibid., pp. 906–909.

5. Ibid., p. 913.

6. See "Mirror of Perfection," trans. Leo Sherley-Price, in *Omnibus*, p. 1230.

7. Thomas of Celano, "The First Life of St. Francis," trans. Placid Hermann, O.F.M., in *Omnibus*, p. 274.

8. See Thomas of Celano, "The Second Life of St.

Francis," trans. Placid Hermann, O.F.M., in *Omnibus*, pp. 530–531.

9. Miriam Ottenberg, "A Song in Her Heart for Multiple Sclerosis," *The Washington Star*, August 8, 1976.

10. Ernest Kurtz, "Why A.A. Works: The Intellectual Significance of Alcoholics Anonymous," *Journal of Studies on Alcohol*, Vol. 43, No. 1 (1982), pp. 38–80.

ILLUMINATIONBOOKS

Other Books in the Series

Little Pieces of Light...Darkness and Personal Growth
by Joyce Rupp

Lessons from the Monastery That Touch Your Life
by M. Basil Pennington, O.C.S.O.

As You and the Abused Person Journey Together
by Sharon E. Cheston

Spirituality, Stress & You
by Thomas E. Rodgerson

Joy, The Dancing Spirit of Love Surrounding You
by Beverly Elaine Eanes

Every Decision You Make Is a Spiritual One
by Anthony J. De Conciliis with John F. Kinsella

Celebrating the Woman You Are
by S. Suzanne Mayer, I.H.M.

Why Are You Worrying?
by Joseph W. Ciarrocchi

Partners in the Divine Dance of Our Three Person'd God
by Shaun McCarty, S.T.